COLLECTION ONE

COLLECTION ONE

GETTING UP EARLY

BRENDAN KENNELLY

1966

ALLEN *Af* FIGGIS

DUBLIN

*Made and printed in the Republic of
Ireland by Cahill and Co., Ltd., Dublin*

Acknowledgment is made to the editors of *The Dublin Magazine*, *The Irish Times*, *The Sunday Independent* and *Icarus*, in which some of these poems have been published

CONTENTS

In memory of
Michael O'Donovan

The Gift

It came slowly.
Afraid of insufficient self-content,
Or some inherent weakness in itself,
Small and hesitant,
Like children at the tops of stairs,
It came through shops, rooms, temples,
Streets, places that were badly-lit,
It was a gift that took me unawares,
And I accepted it.

I

Brown bag bulging with faded nothings;
A ticket for three pounds one and six
To Euston, London via Holyhead:
Young faces limp, misunderstanding
What the first gay promptings meant—
A pass into a brilliant wilderness,
A Capital of hopeless promise.
Well, mount the steps: lug the bag:
Take your place. And out of all the crowd,
Watch the girl in the wrinkled coat,
 Her face half-grey.
 Her first time.

Image

The wet, dead body of a bird
Beneath a lifeless stone:
The wish: the face: the life: the word:
The man alone.

A tangled briar, a bleeding hand,
A berry on a bed of ants,
A boy who sips at fear,
A torn pants.

Before Leaving . . .

Before leaving, say something; speak of the long, wet
Fingers of rain that probed the whiteness of your face,
As you walked, head into the frail February light,
Beyond the heaving city's distant rim.
Say a word or two; tell why you set
Your step in muted strength to walk a place
Where silence sprawled across a dim
Line of houses, leaning against the night.
A word about the sand that crept
Against the grasses in the Summer haze;
About the time that trickled by
Unnoticed into angry Winter days;
About the flooding life that swept
That anger Aprilwards to die.
Say something then, before
Leaving. A word or two. No more.

The After-Child

The red heart of the wild boy
Loved the line of trees in the stormy glen,
Loved the mad songs of the tinker-men
And the thin rain of joy.
He could not avoid the hour to brood
On why the growing ghost
Found peace and pleasure most
In solitude.

He hated quarrelling, and knew
That all self-pity, armouring his power
With its small fierceness for an hour,
Clung damp as evening dew.
He saw life caught in a stony road,
In iron, hard and black;
He bent, took on his back,
The broken load.

Mind held a tired woman, so
Pale near the window where the sun came free
On frosted September mornings. She
Was beautiful, but oh
The lined tiredness that filled her face.
Afar, he stared at her,
The red heart hard astir
At wordless grace.

In the small homes of the poor,
He saw their proud humility in bread,
Where hope became small words unsaid,
Love, white ash on the floor.

A shrunken woman had held them all;
She carried life alone,
While it made half-heard moan
Within her shawl.

Groping towards the morning light,
He found small shadows on the sandy grass,
Where light-winged linnets dipped to pass
In curving high their flight.
Time was the noon of a windy day,
And all it had of truth
Was white food for the youth
Along his way.

Time was never right nor wrong;
Eternity was there, in voice, in look,
In ailing letters of a book,
And in a drunkard's song:
He watched it as through a rainy glass,
And when it stood, as though
Bidding him come or go,
He let it pass.

He let it pass. All he heard,
He sifted first, then kept it in his heart,
Pondering on each little part,
Till it became a Word.
He thought still of trees and stormy glen,
And, looking at wet stone,
He made his way alone,
Like other men.

The coldness that is water in the hour before the dawn;
Small girls in a side-street, faces held in hands
Softer than silence; noon-day dark; white night-light;
The broad hush round the pool where lean bulrushes sprout
And herons stand in water, covering young sands;
All, all became the force that lifewards drove his plight.
—Oh let him build his house of faith and doubt.

When was it first? Walking the green ways, round the
        edge of days
Grown into hills of water? Reaching deep, deep
Into the green of moss, drawing the blind down
On life's vague face, pale vision shall conclusions flout?
Or in small things that the impotent heart felt creep
Into a plan, forever held? In lights that drown?
—Oh let him build his house of faith and doubt.

He saw it once or twice: when the frail bull-calf, stumbling,
        fell
On the spiky light of evening, gored in wet
Grass, trembling in the white spirals of its breath;
When the broken bird rose, speared from the bracken, out
Into the air that, man-like, hastened to forget.
Twice. Tremor of limb, quiver of wing. Cold of death.
—Oh let him build his house of faith and doubt.

The vision arches upwards, pale vision known in young
        leaves;
Overarching all — dream, search and seeker. He
Stands now, looking at it, finding shadows, lights,

That are but part. Summers fade. Waters die in drought,
But, in the sunset, streams go spinning to the sea.
Meaning is in winter, life's walls that block our sights.
—The man has built his house of faith and doubt.

Sonnet

The negro smiled. His teeth showed white as snow.
His eyes stirred like the depths of muddy wine.
He said, "Back in Jamaica, I use' go
Pick coconut every mawnin'. Sun shine
Early, five, six o'clock maybe, an' we
Spend all day hackin'. Jus' hackin', man. Fine
Time we have, though. Sometimes, under a tree,
I sleep during day: always watch for sign
Of sun. Man, it was warm. At night, I lie
On sand with girl. Toss her hair. Laugh. And we
Sing a li'l. Now, she have ten chil'ren. I
Know she ugly now, like my mother." He
Paused and smiled again. "My mother fine. But
Man, she think whole world made of coconut."

A Drowned Girl

Waves' delicate fingers twined a tight noose of death around
Her beautiful body, destined, until then, to thrive;
When they scrambled her on to the rocks, she looked so
    young
You'd swear she was still alive.

She didn't look dead, but looked like any other girl
At whom you'd throw an admiring glance;
Quick brightness in a street, disturbing surprise at evening,
Frail truth in the impulse of the dance.

Heroisms happened swiftly; an old man, with bleeding toes,
Attempted things impossible alike to old and young;
Blew his stale breath between her frigid lips,
Too feeble to help stopped heart and water-stifled lung.

Doctor, priest, civilian prayed and probed and tried
To find one reassuring remnant of breath,
As if they couldn't see why a girl in a green swimsuit
Should be so irretrievably stretched in death.

There was no flood-tide of grief then, no cold consciousness
Of the essential tragedy, yet;
But the curious gaped, mumbled and stumbled
In a way impossible to forget.

Awareness wrapped itself like wet ropes of weed around
    the minds of all,
Rocks and beach became a mesmerized room,
And she, turning cold, looked somehow unwanted,
A blue child thrust from an impatient womb.

Various doctors pronounced her dead and everyone stood
    aside
While stretcher-bearers carried her from the rocks to a house
    on dry land;
Shortly afterwards, waves' delicate fingers twined white
    ribbons of foam
Around her footprints, perfect in the gentle sand . . .

Farmer

Weather's fist has knuckled him
Into incredibly stoic hardness;
Through cloudy gaps, he scans the sky
Waiting for promise.

Bull calves, clay, trampled crops—
These trouble his blood;
Slow seasons inculcate
A saving fortitude.

Angular, ungainly,
Beyond his momentary prime,
He legs it like a weary cob
Through the unprofitable fields of time.

Granted, the body of clay,
Limp, anonymous, blind,
Who would venture to say what stirs
In the dim stables of his mind?

Do not dismiss him, then.
He endures, wedded to fields and grass.
History trudges by.
He sees it pass.

Children's Hospital

Huge-headed, this petrified freak of clay
Stares at the staring visitors bearing flowers,
Fragrant tokens of a mute desire to see
The prone ones on the highway to recovery.
Recovery? This one, girl, five years stretched,
Looks and looks and says
Nothing. Behind her eyes,
Bright mornings of her body's freedom.

Intruding rays of sunlight bring
The sky's immaculate benediction
On suffering
That happens in the dullest way
While innumerable children blunder towards
The dangerous light of day.

While things endure or break, while winter comes again
And prowls morosely through dark places,
I read the clammy script of pain
On children's faces.
In Ward 11, Unit 4, St. Mary's Hospital,
Neatly-arranged, paralysed creation
Lies limp between the lime-white sheets.

Intruding sunlight hovers on
The unfathomable fruit of God's imagination.

And now, in the littered desolation of the street,
The Brown Man's woman stands, suckling her small
Child in the huddled darkness of her shawl;
Who would have thought such love would be complete?
It could be a grimed, swashbuckling brat,
A shifty beggar or an airy boy
Who'd gallivant green townlands out of devilment or joy,
—But her love is none the less for that.

Love's mystery, seen thus, is best;
That the Brown Man's furtive wife, for whom
Life rippled in deep rivers of her womb,
Should feel life shuddering her breast.
God moulded her in softness, as of silk,
He gave her will, and laughter, and power
To net a leaping heart in a short hour,
And then, for men unborn, He gave her milk.

Deeper, this, than darknesses of history,
Than shuttered secrets, silence unexplained,
Than Solomon's wise head that so well reigned
Through one tremendous hour of glory.
Paved village underneath, wild sky above,
The Brown Man's woman, two in one,
Through mortal milk has long begun
To make immortal legends of her love.

The Birds

Beneath the stare of God's gold burning eye,
Two crisp hands clap; a thousand plover rise
And wheel across the clean meadows of the sky.

Black wings flash and gleam; a perfect white
Makes beautiful each rising breast,
Sovereign in the far-off miracle of flight.

Their terror is a lovely thing,
A sudden inspiration, exploding
In the thunder of each beating wing;

A startling rout, as of an army driven
In broken regiments
Against the proud, fantastic face of heaven.

And yet, no mad disorder, no raucous accident
Deforms the miracle; high flocks
Fulfil an inbred, furious intent.

In screams of dread, perfection whirls
Along the headlands of the sky;
They circle, gabbing now like girls,

And wing to safety in Carrig Wood,
Dip through branches, disappear; across the sky,
The pale sun throws a quilt of solitude.

After terror, they are safety's prisoners,
Momentary victims of security
In labyrinths where surly winter stirs.

They breathe on branches, hidden and alone.
Fear will flare again, but now the abandoned sky
Is turning cold and grey as stone.

I think about that marvellous rout, that empty sky,
That flight of plover hidden from
The stare of God's gold burning eye.

The Way of Waves

Now they are arching their fabulous backs,
Angry as cats in the half-light of evening,
Flinging vehement foam on unbreakable rocks.

Their ramshackle thunder bawls in the caves,
White puddles of froth spatter the cliff-tops,
Wild keening resounds in the Nine Daughters' Graves.

We stand above waves, beneath us they break,
While God's spittle whitens the lonely sand-dunes;
Do they gather and break for our sake, or whose sake?

Relentless, they hurtle their brutal tirade
At pebble and shingle, appalling sea-slime
From which we, above wave-tops, at first light were made.

Sight fails with the coming of night; the ignorant roar
Magnifies, yet seems remote; white hooves
Of confusion beat hard on the shore.

The Dummies

Their restless hands articulate desire
In frantic gestures of meaning,
Fantastic patterns of the inner fire.

So it must have been among the first
Brothers—a frenzy of excitement
Before love, hate, hunger, thirst

Were named. Four dummies! Brothers too !
Each one in his particular silence
Creates bridges, trees, deep spaces through

Which he reaches to a brother, hungrily.
Outer beasts move in colourful confusion.
Brothers need each other, utterly.

The spirit's energy is their eloquence. Their
Animated hands mould marvellous
Expressions out of the simple air.

Yet, each one's unalterable separateness remains.
In tragic silence, each dumb soul
Is islanded in darkness of the city lanes.

Old Men

They share the sun's enormous charity
This summer morning; old lame-leg, one hand
Hanging dead, shuffles past the flowers and
Greenery; one swaddled in anonymity,
A handkerchief across his face; another
Gobbling yesterday's news with his remaining eye;
A countryman—old scarecrow—emits a sigh
Of desolation. Solitary, they sit together
In common sunlight, the only thing
They share, apart from feebleness. I see
A tourist striding past the refuse of humanity,
His camera cocked and ready. He sees
Old men, simply sitting and expecting
What-you-will. He eyes the young, upspringing trees.

The Shannon

Brown-legged girl and boy win seagrass
From the resolute rocks;
Their tiny figures move like birds
Beside the treacherous tranquillity of waves.
On this, the Kerry coast,
Peace hovers like an accusation
Over the unlaboured land;
Eloquent silence commemorates
The pointless scattering of love.
Between the Banner County and the Kingdom
The burly Shannon strides into the sea.
In rocky desolation, the unploughed parishes end;
The outnumbering waves insist
That the river is nobody's friend.

Moloney at the Wake

"That was the gay night," he said,
"I went to a wake and hopped into bed
With the corpse; not a very nice
Thing to do, I suppose; cold as ice
Her belly and thighs;
Two brown pennies covered her eyes;
They'd tied up her foxy hair
And crossed her hands as though in prayer.
When alive, the same girl wasn't much
Given to prayers and such,
But they made her look as though she could
Have prayed the legs from under God.
Anyway, I got into bed
There and then beside the dead
Woman; a disastrous
Thing to do because the whole house
Thought I was mad. I drew a long
Breath, looked at her and broke into song.
With her icy belly against my knee
I sang 'Why don't you answer me'.
Christ, man, talk of a scatter! The whole place
Panicked; 'tis a terrible disgrace,
They said, when a drunken sot like you
Can stagger in here through
The open door, and without an attempt at a **prayer**
Make a wild buck-lepp in there
Beside herself, and she stretched.
                              Never mind, I said,
What do you, or I, know of the dead?
Of course, I grant that politeness must be **shown**
At all times, so I'll get up now and leave her **alone**.

Two mugs o' porter, a quick Hail Mary for the dead,
Then I hit for home and the wife in bed."

He finished; raised his pint to leathery lips,
And waited for the heart's eclipse.

"O she was the handsome corpse," he said,
"Divil a difference between livin' and dead
You'd see in her; a fine red face
On a starchy pillow edged with lace,
Her cold hands clasped, her mousy hair
As neatly tied as a girl's at a fair.
Touchin' forty she was when she passed away,
But twenty she looked as she lay
In bed on the broad of her back.
Kate Finucane of Asdee West
Was stretched in death, but she looked her best!

      Her cousins had come
From all parts of the Kingdom
For the wake; Coffeys and Lanes from Dingle,
McCarthys and Ryans, married and single,
Honest and otherwise. For a day and a night
As she lay in her bed, a sight
For sore eyes, they drank and they prayed
And they sang her to heaven—as fine
A wake as ever I went to in all my time!

Well, there was nothin' to do, after prayin' and drinkin',
But lift herself into the coffin.
'Twas at that moment, glory to God,
As I stood with my glass at the head
Of her bed, that she stretched like a cat and opened her eyes
And lifted her head in great surprise;
And motherogod will I ever forget
The cut an' the go, the sight an' the set
Of her when, calm as you like, with a toss of her head,
Kate Finucane sat up in the bed!

                              No need to tell
Of all the confusion that fell
On the cousins, neighbours, myself and the house.
Dead she'd been, and now this disastrous
Return to life, upsettin' the whole
Place, and I thinkin' her body was lackin' a soul.
But after a while, things quietened down
And Kate made tea for the cousins. She found
She'd not seen them for ages. What's more,
She clapped her eye on a Lenamore
Man called Harty, and three months later,
Paraded him in rare style up to the altar!
On top o' that, she showed the world she could
Make a dandy wife, for she's still to the good,
And without doubt or favour, fright or fear,
Kate Finucane has a child a year!

"Gay woman, Kate," Moloney said,
"Divil a difference between livin' and dead!"

"My soul from hell, the night the ould **wan** died,"
Moloney said, "I cried and cried
Tears down. I'd been tied to her string
Through rack and hardship and the wild fling
Of youth, through manhood and the grey
Days when youth begins to slip away,
And now my addled heart and head
Were bound by the memory o' the dead.

Well, anyway, after puttin' herself down
In the box, I went to the town
O' Lishtowel for a few drinks, and there
I met a Knockanore woman with red hair
And gamey eye. I made bold
And in a short time had told
Her my story. She cocked her ear and listened well.
We drank until the darkness fell
And for hours after. The talk
Spun on love. 'Can I walk
A piece with you?' says I. 'Moloney,' says she,
'You're welcome to do what you like with me.'
Fair enough! We left Lishtowel and struck the road,
Footin' it free over pothole
And gravel. The Knockanore woman was full o' guff
And harped on all the tricks o' love.
I upped with the question. She
Was willin' and free.
'Where would you like it?' says I. 'Well,' she said,
'God's green earth is a warm bed.'

'Right you are, girl,' says I.
It happened we were passin' by
Gale graveyard where my mother lay.
'What would you say
To this place?' says I. 'Moloney,' says she,
'If it's right with you, it's right with me.'

Straightaway, I opened the gate and led
The Knockanore woman over the dead
O' seven parishes. Talk of a flyer!
Fast as they come and hot as fire!
She fell down on the soft clay
Of a fresh grave, and before I could say
A word, I was on the ground as well,
Goin' like the hammers o' hell!
'Twas only then I saw where I was.
On my mother's grave! But that was no cause
For panic, though I was a bit
Upset at first by the strangeness of it.
The Knockanore woman was happy as Larry,
And I was sparkin' and merry
As a cricket. 'Yerra, you might
As well enjoy the gift o' the night
While you have the chance,' I said
To myself, realizin' the dead are dead,
Past holiness and harms—
And the livin' woman was in my arms.

'Twas great fun
While it lasted, and it lasted long. The sun
Was startin' to climb the sky when we rose
Up and settled our clothes.

'How are you, girl,' says I.
'Yerra, fine,' says she.
' 'Twas a fine night,' says I.
' 'Twas so, but a bit cold towards mornin',' says she,
'And I wouldn't mind a hot cup o' tay
This minute.' 'Whist,' I said,
Suddenly remembering the quiet dead.
With the memory, I started to sing,
Then and there, a bar of a jig,
And as I sang I danced as well
On the body whose soul was in heaven or hell.
'You're a gay man,' says she, 'to bring
Me to a place like this for your bit of a fling,
And I'm thinkin' the love has gone to your head
When you dance a jig on the bones o' the dead.'
Said I, 'By the Christ that is divine,
If I have a son may he dance on mine.
While a man has a chance he should dance and sing,'
    I said,
'For he'll be the hell of a long time dead.
So come on now without further ado
And I'll put on the kettle for the tay.'
She smiled and we started on our way
In the early light that was breaking for day.

The night was lost, the daylight stretched ahead,
Behind me lay the unforgettable dead,
Beside me walked a woman with gamey eye,
Laughing as the sun rose in the sky."

My Dark Fathers

My dark fathers lived the intolerable day
Committed always to the night of wrong,
Stiffened at the hearthstone, the woman lay,
Perished feet nailed to her man's breastbone.
Grim houses beckoned in the swelling gloom
Of Munster fields where the Atlantic night
Fettered the child within the pit of doom,
And everywhere a going down of light.

And yet upon the sandy Kerry shore
The woman once had danced at ebbing tide
Because she loved flute music—and still more
Because a lady wondered at the pride
Of one so humble. That was long before
The green plant withered by an evil chance;
When winds of hunger howled at every door
She heard the music dwindle and forgot the dance.

Such mercy as the wolf receives was hers
Whose dance became a rhythm in a grave,
Achieved beneath the thorny savage furze
That yellowed fiercely in a mountain cave.
Immune to pity, she, whose crime was love,
Crouched, shivered, searched the threatening sky,
Discovered ready signs, compelled to move
Her to her innocent appalling cry.

Skeletoned in darkness, my dark fathers lay
Unknown, and could not understand
The giant grief that trampled night and day,
The awful absence moping through the land.

Upon the headland, the encroaching sea
Left sand that hardened after tides of Spring,
No dancing feet disturbed its symmetry
And those who loved good music ceased to sing.

Since every moment of the clock
Accumulates to form a final name,
Since I am come of Kerry clay and rock,
I celebrate the darkness and the shame
That could compel a man to turn his face
Against the wall, withdrawn from light so strong
And undeceiving, spancelled in a place
Of unapplauding hands and broken song.

Certain Old Women

Like ancient shrunken dolls they shuffle by
And amble dumbly into shops or bars,
Are never exquisitely nervous now
But withered stoics after casual wars.

Moving towards the unfathomable dark
Through fragments of a necessary light,
They sit by the canal or in the park
On mornings, evenings; and they wait for night.

They're mostly shapeless. Jowls dangle, tight lips
Purse or mutter, soft dugs flap and fall;
Flesh dries on shoulders, buttocks, thighs and hips,
Yet, curiously, at the end of all,

I think that they, wry puppets in the game,
Surviving every need of love and pence,
Go awkwardly as beggars, ages lame,
Into a transcendental innocence.

Johnny Gobless

Gaunt, ungracious in the rain,
Fingering a silver chain,
He goes stalking up and down
Blessing the unwieldy town.

Madness glitters in his eyes,
Weight of sacred sympathies,
And from his lips explode, like birds,
Flocks of rapid frightened words.

I think of lonely William Blake
Who did a world make, re-make,
Who hounded truth until it cried
And laid its head against his side,

Whose discontent was made and given
By the amazing hand of heaven,
Whose deep divine unhappiness
Could only bless, could only bless,

As now this gaunt disordered man
In holy madness, knows he can
Bless the city in the rain
Fingering a silver chain.

Who but poet or madman could
Affirm that all there is, is good?
Or with the truth of passion tell
That heaven holds out its hands to hell?

The fascinated waters roll
With dark deliberate intent,
Stained by flung débris
And excrement.

Ebb and flow until
The high springtide has thinned
Emerging mud; Plato,
Christ, Socrates—drowned in the wind.

The purged city lingers
Under the fierce bowl;
Onwards, backwards, onwards
The fascinated waters roll.

Getting Up Early

Getting up early promises well;
　　A milkhorse on the road
Induces thoughts of a sleeping world
　　And a waking God.

This hour has something sacred;
　　Bells will be ringing soon,
But now I am content to watch
　　The day begin to bloom.

I would only waste my breath
　　On poor superfluous words;
How perfectly they sing for me—
　　The new invisible birds

Who celebrate the light that spreads
　　Like love to window sills,
As morning steps like a laughing girl
　　Down from the Dublin hills.

The Blind Man

Dark from birth,
And therefore spared the shock
Of losing light, not having known its worth.
I am aware of darkness round the clock,
A velvet kingdom, limits undefined,
Where touch, smell, ear equip me well.
Fastidiously, I try the noisy grind,
The aimless gusto of external hell.

I walk the inner alleys night and day,
Explore the salty laneways of the blood,
Note weeds and grasses, refuse thrown away,
Deduce what's evil, beautiful or good.
I move down sidestreets of the marrowbone,
Go moodily along its thoroughfare
On which the sun has sometimes shone;
And therefore I am blithe and debonair.

I've been informed of the things I miss:
Birds that steadily attempt the air,
Peculiar tints of whiskey in a glass,
Surprising sunlight in a woman's hair;
Shells half-buried in the sand
Originally spawned at sea,
Nature's gayest finery and
Casual phenomena of every day.

But vision is not simply seeing straight,
And things discoverable without exist within;
My shells and birds are different, yet elate
Me utterly. Images that spin

Within these limits are my own,
With colours, shapes and forms that I create,
Discovered somewhere in the blood and bone—
I only see whatever I can make.

Therefore I accept dark privacy;
I move beyond each voice
Which, unaware, asserts I cannot see.
While they acclaim, reproach, commend, rejoice,
I go among them, prodding the strange air,
Awkwardly involved while still outside,
Conscious of the things I'm fit to share,
Acknowledging the light I've been denied.

I've seen the incoming government of light
Disestablishing darkness in my room,
And been surprised at the inevitable sight
Of those familiar shapes and forms that come
Into their own, unaltered by the night;
Walls with pictures, mirror, window, door
Reveal themselves, and the awakened blood,
Released from its own dark, pursues once more
Those simple possibilities of good
That make the ruling light of everyday
A brief bewilderment to be endured,
Outgoing imperceptibly as work
And systematic hours prepare the way
For the sure tyranny that is restored
With the return of the elected dark.

Winter Night

To-night we talked of wars;
Walking home
Under the wintry stars,
(Their inaccessible light, in lucid cruelty,
Become shuddering emblems of fright),
I watch the desperate clouds and moon.

Who will survive
The dark at noon?

Marlowe

There was a quarrel about the bill
Of reckoning, not paid until
Kit Marlowe, knifed above the eye
By Ingram Frazier, finally
Settled everything with his blood.
The whole account was closed for good.

It was a giant heart that fell
The victim of a tavern brawl.
Young Kit Marlowe met his doom
In a smoky upstairs room.
The blood that flowed was poetry
Unformed by the quick alchemy
That fashioned Faustus in his prime
And followed the fantastic dream
Of Tamburlaine, but was unmade
By the sharp flash of Frazier's blade.

The dark impenetrable past
Remains the scene of tragic waste;
Wasted wisdom, blood and bone
Impoverish the mind of man.
The tragic pity of what is lost
Makes us the living dispossessed;
We inherit but a part
Of the rich flux, preserved in art,
And therefore every single soul
Is ultimately less than whole.
Present poverty derives
From the curse of wasted lives.

The dead creator on the floor
Has spoken well and must endure,
Surviving hands that ruin and waste
Incessantly, till all seems lost.

It is impossible to tell
How tragic is the unpaid bill,
Or guess at what was left unsaid
When the blood poured from Marlowe's head.

The Tamer

Man and stallion are the scene;
Man steps behind
The grey brute, the rein
Conducting mastery
In his patient hand;
Gods of power ply,

Impartial yet, between the two;
The watchful man
Moves shrewdly through
Necessary stages of his rule;
Touch, word and attitude combine,
Promise to make him masterful.

The light rein links him with the brute;
His head held high
(As the stallion's is, the white
Star splendid on the forehead),
His hands stretch forth as though
Supplicating the animal blood.

Proudly the stallion steps it out,
His nervous back
Unsaddled, his shining mane uncut;
Nostrils quiver, feet still unshod
Prance, shudder, crack
The silence of the road.

The tamer murmurs along the air
"Hi, beast! Hi, beast!"

Determined now to master
Brute muscle and bone,
Achieve the whip-hand in the test,
Subdue the strong paragon.

Tense they go together now,
The stallion's head
Almost imperceptibly
Obeys the least flick of the rein,
Subtlest impulses conveyed
By the commanding man.

"Hi, beast! Hi, beast!"—on many a road
These words are said
Gently to pacify the blood
Unsubmissive still
To the hand that soon bends power and pride
To its own will.

Lislaughtin Abbey

Flashing starlings twist and turn
   In the sky above my head,
While in Lislaughtin Abbey lie
   The packed anticipating dead.

Silent generations there
   That long had bent the knee
Endow the Shannon with the grace
   Of reaching to the sea.

Swollen by the rich juice of the dead,
   The Shannon moves with ease
Towards a mighty union with
   Atlantic mysteries.

But though the river sweeps beyond
   Each congested bone,
Its currents do not swirl towards
   A resurrection,

Any more than starlings do
   That, fearing death this winter day,
Create small thunder in the sky
   And shelter where they may,

Ignoring green Lislaughtin where
   Subtle shadows pass
Through shattered altars, broken walls,
   The blood of martyrs in the grass,

Into the ground that winters well
  And blossoms soon or late,
Preserving patient multitudes
  Who are content to wait

Till they at last disturb the stones,
  The fox's lair, the starling's nest,
To cry out with the howling damned,
  To wonder with the Blessed,

To hear the word for which they wait
  Under the coarse grass
The meanest blade of which assists
  In what must come to pass,

To see why silent centuries
  Have finally sufficed
To purge all in the rising flood
  Of the overflowing blood of Christ.

Restless at the gate, I turn away
  Groping towards what can't be said
And know I know but little
  Of the birds, the river and the dead.

Spring in Kerry

Hungry tides recede and on the shore
These rocks survive the February flood;
Whatever's past, whatever lies in store
Is now, it seems, undoubtedly for good;
The yellow whins emerge in Knockanore,
A curlew, cocky in the Shannon mud,
Foraging, indicates the closing door
Of winter, and deep in Bambury's wood

Rebellion stirs, as though imprisoned things,
Burdened with darkness but aware of light,
Sensing a possible brilliance in the gloom,

Threw off all chains, defeated posturings,
And like a blind man privileged with sight
Rejoiced at all the elemental bloom.

A Farmer Thinks of his Daft Son

Like any ass I have to bear
A cross upon my back,
An only son half-gone in the head,
Myself upon the rack,
Not knowing when his wiry life
Will suddenly go slack.

How can I tell with certainty
What my son desires?—
Weeds upon the river-bed,
Guidance from the stars,
Praises from the lips of fools,
Truth from the lips of liars,
Women rising Phoenix-like
Out of their spent fires.

Thinking that I'll find him
Stretched outside in the shed,
Or wet and stiff in a boggy pool
God knows how long dead,
I twist and turn the whole night long
In a sleepless bed.

The Good

(For Eavan)

The good are vulnerable
As any bird in flight,
They do not think of safety,
Are blind to possible extinction
And when most vulnerable
Are most themselves.
The good are real as the sun,
Are best perceived through clouds
Of casual corruption
That cannot kill the luminous sufficiency
That shines on city, sea and wilderness,
Fastidiously revealing
One man to another,
Who yet will not accept
Responsibilities of light.
The good incline to praise,
To have the knack of seeing that
The best is not destroyed
Although forever threatened.
The good go naked in all weathers,
And by their nakedness rebuke
The small protective sanities
That hide men from themselves.
The good are difficult to see
Though open, rare, destructible;
Always, they retain a kind of youth,
The vulnerable grace
Of any bird in flight,
Content to be itself,
Accomplished master and potential victim,
Accepting what the earth or sky intends.
I think that I know one or two
Among my friends.

Light Dying

In Memoriam Frank O'Connor (Michael O'Donovan)

Climbing the last steps to your house, I knew
That I would find you in your chair,
Watching the light die along the canal,
Recalling the glad creators, all
Who'd played a part in the miracle;
A silver-haired remembering king, superb there
In dying light, all ghosts being at your beck and call,
You made them speak as only you could do,

Of generosity or loneliness or love
Because, you said, all men are voices, heard
In the pure air of the imagination.
I hear you now, your rich voice deep and kind,
Rescuing a poem from time, bringing to mind
Lost centuries with a summoning word,
Lavishing on us who need much more of
What you gave, glimpses of heroic vision.

So you were angry at the pulling down
Of what recalled a finer age; you tried
To show how certain things destroyed, ignored,
Neglected was a crime against the past,
Impoverished the present. Some midland town
Attracted you, you stood in the waste
Places of an old church and, profoundly stirred,
Pondered how you could save what time had sorely tried,

Or else you cried in rage against the force
That would reduce to barren silence all
Who would articulate dark Ireland's soul;
You knew the evil of the pious curse,

47

The hearts that make God pitifully small
Until He seems the God of little fear
And not the God that you desired at all;
And yet you had the heart to do and dare.

I see you standing at your window,
Lifting a glass, watching the dying light
Along the quiet canal bank come and go
Until the time has come to say good-night:
You see me to the door; you lift a hand
Half-shyly, awkwardly, while I remark
Your soul's fine courtesy, my friend, and
Walk outside, alone, suddenly in the dark.

But in the dark or no, I realise
Your life's transcendent dignity,
A thing more wonderful than April skies
Emerging in compelling majesty,
Leaving mad March behind and making bloom
Each flower outstripping every weed and thorn;
Life rises from the crowded clay of doom,
Light dying promises the light re-born.